THE LIBRARY OF
AMERICAN
LIVES AND TIMES™

COMMODORE MATTHEW PERRY

and the Perry Expedition to Japan

David G. Wittner

The Rosen Publishing Group's
PowerPlus Books™
New York

Published in 2005 by The Rosen Publishing Group, Inc.
29 East 21st Street, New York, NY 10010

First Edition

Editor's Note: All quotations have been reproduced as they appeared in the letters and diaries from which they were borrowed. No correction was made to the inconsistent spelling that was common in that time period.

Library of Congress Cataloging-in-Publication Data

Wittner, David G.
Commodore Matthew Perry and the Perry Expedition to Japan / David G. Wittner.— 1st ed.
  p. cm. — (The library of American lives and times)
Summary: Surveys the life of Matthew Perry, a naval officer from a seafaring family, whose accomplishments are many but who is best remembered for opening Japan to trade with other nations.
Includes bibliographical references and index.
ISBN 1-4042-2645-1
1. Perry, Matthew Calbraith, 1794–1858—Juvenile literature. 2. Admirals—United States—Biography—Juvenile literature. 3. United States—History, Naval—To 1900—Juvenile literature. 4. United States. Navy—Biography—Juvenile literature. 5. United States Naval Expedition to Japan (1852–1854)—Juvenile literature. [1. Perry, Matthew Calbraith, 1794–1858. 2. Admirals. 3. United States—History, Naval—To 1900. 4. United States. Navy—Biography. 5. United States Naval Expedition to Japan (1852–1854)] I. Title. II. Series.
E182.P44 W57 2005
327.73052'09'034—dc22

                              2003015516

Manufactured in the United States of America

CONTENTS

1. The Newport Perrys

Matthew Calbraith Perry is best known as the American naval officer who opened Japan to the world in 1853. Perry also accomplished other things in his life that deserve remembrance. He rose through the ranks of the U.S. Navy and served during the War of 1812. He hunted pirates in the West Indies and slave traders in the Mediterranean Sea. He helped to establish African American settlements in Africa and fought in the Mexican War. In Japan, Perry demonstrated that he was a good negotiator when he signed a treaty with the Japanese government in 1854.

Perry's family has been called one of the United States' first naval families. To understand how the Perrys received this title and to see how Perry was influenced by his family background, it is important to look back to the first Perry who came to this country. In 1639, Edward

---

Opposite: This photograph of Commodore Matthew Calbraith Perry was taken between 1854 and 1858 by Mathew Brady. The photograph appeared on Perry's *carte-de-visite,* or calling card, which was a popular item in the mid-nineteenth century.

Perry, Matthew's great-great-grandfather, left England and came to Sandwich, Massachusetts. Edward Perry was a member of a religious order known as the Quakers. He left England to escape religious persecution, but unfortunately found little tolerance in the Massachusetts colony.

Matthew Perry's great-grandfather, Benjamin, moved from Massachusetts to Rhode Island in 1704 because he had heard that Quakers were welcome there. He found that he fit well into Rhode Island society. He bought land

This 1849 painting shows a Quaker religious service, which is called a meeting. Quakers are also known as the Society of Friends. The church began in the mid-seventeenth century in England and was known for its belief in pacifism and its tolerance of other religions.

and accumulated a good deal of wealth. Benjamin and his wife, Susannah, had five children. Their third son, Freeman Perry, was Matthew Perry's grandfather. Freeman was a doctor and a surveyor, and he served as chief justice of Rhode Island's courts during the American Revolution. Freeman Perry did not fight in the American Revolution because of the Quaker belief in pacifism. He would be the last of the "peaceful Perrys," however.

Matthew Perry's father, Christopher Perry, son of Freeman Perry, broke with the family's Quaker tradition. At the age of fourteen or fifteen, he began a long military career when he joined the Kingston Reds, a militia unit, so that he could fight in the American Revolution. After an incident that forced many men in the militia unit to flee Kingston, Christopher went to Boston, where he signed up to serve on a Yankee privateer. A privateer is a privately owned ship licensed to attack enemy ships during times of war. Privateers also hunted down, captured, and sold enemy merchant vessels, which is how the captain got the money to pay the crew.

Christopher Perry served on a number of privateers and on two Continental naval vessels. Christopher was happy as long as he was able to fight for the cause of American independence. Christopher's service record and adventurous spirit earned him the title of the first "fighting Perry." His long career and his many exploits were a source of inspiration for his children.

It was on one of his tours of duty aboard a privateer that Christopher first saw his future wife. In June 1780, Christopher's ship was captured by the British navy off the coast of Ireland. He was thrown into jail as a prisoner of war but was released after a short time. One night Christopher spotted a beautiful girl and said, "There goes my future wife." A few years later, after the war had ended, Christopher was working on a ship that sailed between Dublin, Ireland, and Philadelphia, Pennsylvania. He discovered that one of the passengers was Sarah Alexander, the woman he had once jokingly said would be his wife. The two got to know each other and were married soon after the ship docked in Philadelphia, in August 1784. The couple moved to the Narragansett area of Rhode Island and Christopher gave up his life as a privateer to become a farmer. Even after the birth of his first son, Oliver Hazard Perry, in 1785, Christopher Perry found that the life of a farmer did not suit him. It lacked the excitement and adventure of a life on the high seas. Eventually, Christopher returned to the sea as a master on a cargo ship.

In the early 1790s, Freeman Perry bought a cozy little house for the young couple in Newport, Rhode Island. Newport was one of the most cosmopolitan cities in the country and the Perrys and their children were in the middle of all the excitement. When Christopher was not at sea, he and Sarah worked on raising a family. After

Documents called Letters of Marque were issued to ships during the American Revolution. These papers gave permission for merchant vessels to seize British merchant ships. This aided the Continental navy, which was fighting against Britain's Royal Navy, then the world's most powerful navy. Howard Pyle painted *An American Privateer Taking a British Prize* for *Harper's Magazine* in 1908.

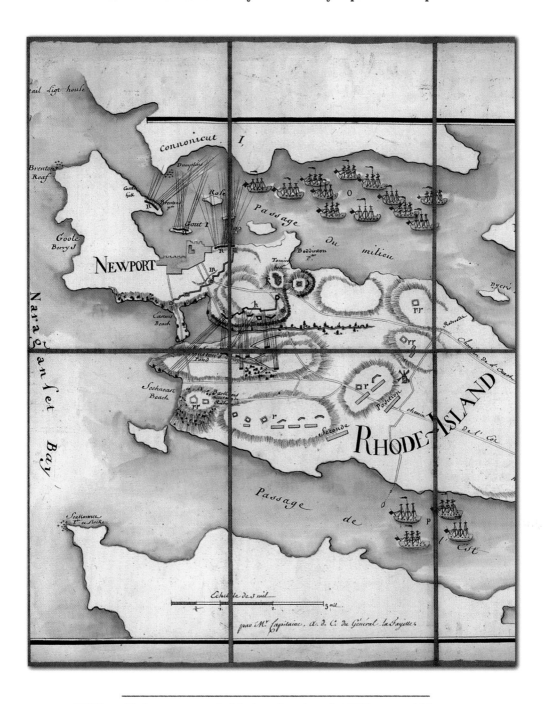

William Faden engraved this hand-colored 1777 map of Newport, Rhode Island. Newport was founded in 1639 by a religious group from Massachusetts. The town had one of the most prosperous ports in the colonies.

Oliver Hazard, they had seven more children. They were Raymond Henry, Sarah Wallace, Matthew James Calbraith, Anna Maria, Jane Tweedy, James Alexander, and Nathaniel Hazard.

Matthew James Calbraith Perry was born on April 10, 1794. Perry had a typical childhood for the time. Living only a short distance from the ocean, he spent his summers playing on the beaches, swimming with friends and watching the ships that sailed in and out of the harbor. In the autumn he hunted in the country-side, and in the winter he skated on frozen ponds. Perry first went to school in a local schoolhouse, and then he attended private school. He was a serious student who spent a lot of time studying.

For much of his life, Perry looked up to his father and his older brother Oliver. Just as they did, he yearned for a life at sea. In 1799, Christopher Perry rejoined the U.S. Navy and became captain of a new ship, the *General Greene*. Oliver followed in his father's footsteps and enlisted at age thirteen, as was common among boys interested in careers in the navy. He served on the *General Greene* as a midshipman and made a name for himself as a young officer.

Life on the *General Greene* was difficult. Diseases such as yellow fever were common. Captain Perry's tour of duty was also marked by disciplinary problems with his men. Sailors could be rowdy when times got hard. Some of the sailors had been caught stealing lobsters in

This portrait of Oliver Hazard Perry (1785–1819) was painted around 1814 by Rembrandt Peale. This was just after Oliver's famous victory over the British navy at Lake Erie in the War of 1812. Perry said of the battle, "We have met the enemy and they are ours."

Newport before the ship set sail. In a seafaring city like Newport, stealing lobsters was a serious crime. Even though these sailors were punished, they continued to cause trouble once the *General Greene* was at sea. Captain Perry tried to discipline the men but nothing seemed to work. When the *General Greene* returned to port, five of these unruly sailors filed charges against Captain Perry for "oppression and cruelty." In a naval court, Captain Perry was acquitted of some of the charges against him, but was found guilty of not maintaining discipline on his ship while at sea.

Captain Perry's problems at sea had a profound effect on young Matthew. Years later, when he received command of his own ship, he was concerned about disease and the health of his crew. He was also a strict captain so that his men would never step out of line. Perry recalled his brother's and father's stories about their time on the *General Greene*. As a young officer, Perry would create policies based on these stories.

2. Perry Takes to the Sea

At age twelve, Matthew Calbraith Perry asked his father for permission to join the navy. Captain Perry agreed that this would be a good career choice. After the boy's thirteenth birthday, Captain Perry helped Matthew obtain a midshipman's position. President Thomas Jefferson signed the orders on January 16, 1809. Matthew was sent to the Brooklyn Navy Yard in Brooklyn, New York, where he received two months' training before being sent to sea. In March 1809, he reported for duty on board the *Revenge*, a twelve-gun schooner commanded by his older brother, Lieutenant Oliver Hazard Perry.

Life was hard for a midshipman during the nineteenth century. "Reefers," as midshipmen were called, lived on the steerage deck. This was under the main deck, just below the ship's waterline, near the rudder. The only light on the steerage deck came from whale-oil lamps, and the only air came from hatches in the main deck that could be left open in good weather. Reefers slept on rope hammocks that swung from hooks screwed into the ship.

As did other officers, midshipmen stood watch and learned naval skills, such as working with rigging, knot tying, rope splicing, sail making, navigation, and gunnery. Young officers were taught mathematics so that they could navigate using the stars and calculate distance. Every ship also had a chaplain, who conducted religious services and taught English composition, French, and international law to the midshipmen. As did other young boys, the midshipmen also liked to fool around. Matthew, however, was a rather serious boy

This painting by George H. Comegys is entitled *A Sailor of the U.S.S. Constitution, Toasting a New Recruit in a Saloon.* In the early nineteenth century, it was not unknown for officers to take new recruits out on the town as a reward for signing up for service.

who remained focused on his goal of becoming a good officer. He did not like to take unnecessary chances. Commodore John Rodgers recognized Matthew's potential and chose him to be his personal aide. This gave Matthew the opportunity to be close to one of the navy's most famous and talented officers. Part of his duty was to keep the ship's official journal, a record of nearly everything that happened on board.

Soon Rodgers received command of another ship, the frigate *President*, and Matthew, who had become Rodgers's aide, was transferred with him. There were four hundred men and officers on the *President*, including Perry's older brother Raymond, who was also a midshipman. Matthew Perry had what was called the Perry luck. Not only was he lucky for being transferred to the fastest, best armed, and newest of the U.S. Navy's ships, but also he was lucky because, not long after he left the *Revenge*, it was caught in a storm and wrecked. A number of sailors were injured or killed.

Matthew Perry's first chance to experience action at sea came in 1811. He was seventeen. Relations between the British and the Americans were becoming tense because of a British naval practice called impressment. Britain, which was at war with France, needed sailors. British ships would board American merchant vessels to

Charles Willson Peale painted this portrait of Commodore John Rodgers (1773–1838) around 1818. When serving as Rodgers's aide, Perry learned about leadership through observing how Rodgers handled his command.

impress, or capture, men and to force them to become members of the British navy. British officials justified this practice because they refused to recognize American citizenship. They considered Americans who had been born in England to be English citizens and deserters from military service. Although impressment was not a serious threat, some members of the U.S. Congress used these issues as evidence for the need to go to war with Britain.

In late April 1811, the *President* received orders to intercept the ship *Guerrière*, a British ship that had been stopping U.S. merchant vessels, looking for sailors to impress. Lookouts on the *President* spotted sails on the horizon and Commodore Rodgers ordered his men to pursue the foreign vessel. The ship they were chasing, however, was not the *Guerrière*. It was the British sloop *Little Belt*. The *Little Belt*'s captain, Arthur Bingham, thought that the *President* was a French merchant vessel and decided to capture it and take its cargo. By the time Bingham realized his mistake, it was too late to avoid a fight. The two ships prepared for battle. An overanxious British sailor on board the *Little Belt* fired a cannon at the American vessel. Commodore Rodgers's crew responded. The two ships blasted away at each other at close range. After fifteen minutes, the *Little Belt*'s guns were destroyed, and the ship's sails and rigging were severely damaged. Even though Captain Bingham had not surrendered, Commodore Rodgers ordered a cease-fire and sailed out to a safe distance. The next morning,

Rodgers sailed back to the *Little Belt* to find out the name of the ship and to offer assistance.

Although it was an American naval victory, the difference in size between the *President*, with forty-four guns, and the *Little Belt*, with twenty guns, meant that the victory brought neither honor nor glory to the young U.S. Navy. Incidents such as these contributed to the escalating hostility between Britain and the United States that would erupt as the War of 1812 one year later.

When U.S. Congress declared war on Britain on June 18, 1812, eighteen-year-old Matthew Perry and the crew of the *President* set sail for the waters of Bermuda. Their orders were to find and capture a large British merchant convoy that sailed regularly between Jamaica and England. At sunrise on June 23, lookouts on the *President* spotted a ship sailing in their direction. It was the British frigate *Belvidera*. The *President* caught up to the *Belvidera* later in the day and opened fire. After hitting the *Belvidera* a number of times, one of the *President*'s guns exploded. One man was killed and thirteen were injured, including Commodore Rodgers and Perry. Perry's injuries were minor, but Rodgers's leg was shattered. The *Belvidera* escaped and the *President* returned to shore for repairs.

This was a rather disappointing start to the war for the U.S. Navy. They had lost the opportunity to score a decisive victory and had sustained a number of injuries and damaged a ship in the process.

Sloop
3 masts, square-rigged

Brig
2 masts, square-rigged

Sailing ships are named according to size, the number of masts, and the types of sails they use. The term "rigging" refers to the ropes and equipment used to support and control the sails and masts, as well as the shape of the sails used on a ship. Fore-and-aft rigged ships have sails that are stretched vertically from the mast, giving them a triangular shape.

Square-rigged ships have sails that are stretched horizontally across the mast, giving them a square shape. A sloop can have one, two, or more masts. All its masts are square-rigged. A brig has two masts, and either one or both of the masts are square-rigged. A schooner has two or more masts. Frigates have three masts, all of which are square-rigged.

Schooner
2 masts, fore-and-aft rigged

Frigate
3 masts, square-rigged

Robert Dodd painted *The U.S.S. Chesapeake approaching the H.M.S. Shannon, during the War of 1812* in 1813. The battle took place near Boston Harbor. The British ship *Shannon* defeated the American ship. Captain Lawrence, the commander of the *Chesapeake*, was killed in the battle. His famous last words were, "Don't give up the ship."

The winter of 1812–1813 was unusually harsh and Boston Harbor froze solid. It was not until April 30, 1813, that the *President* went out to sea again. Although the *President* was able to return to its duties of hunting enemy convoys, it was one of only six American vessels to get out of port. The Royal Navy had begun to blockade the entire East Coast of the United States.

The rest of the war was uneventful for Matthew Perry. After his promotion to the rank of lieutenant in

July 1813, Perry was transferred a few times. He ended up back on the crew of the *President* guarding New York City against invasion, but there was little to do. Perry spent a considerable amount of time ashore, where he became friendly with John Slidell, a well-known New York merchant and banker, and Slidell's family. Perry took special interest in Slidell's daughter, Jane. Throughout the summer and autumn of 1814, Perry and Jane courted each other. They were married on Christmas Eve. This was also the same day that the Treaty of Ghent, the peace treaty ending the War of 1812, was signed.

Almost as soon as the ink had dried on the treaty with Britain, the U.S. Congress declared war on Algiers. For years pirates along the Barbary Coast of North Africa had been attacking American merchant ships, taking their cargoes and selling their crews into slavery. Eventually Congress signed an agreement with the pirates, but, during the war with Britain, the dey of Algiers, a powerful prince and pirate, began capturing American merchant vessels again. When the war ended, Congress ordered two squadrons to sail to Algiers.

Lieutenant Perry gained valuable experience as part of the expedition to Algiers. As second in command of the *Chippewa*, he learned how to command his own ship within a larger squadron. More important, he learned the value of making a show of force to ensure that demands be taken seriously. To show the dey that

the United States meant business, the squadron attacked the Algerian flagship and later threatened two other Algerian leaders so that they would sign and honor treaties. When the two squadrons departed the Mediterranean, four warships were left behind to guard American shipping interests and to make sure the dey of Algiers honored the treaty.

When the *Chippewa* returned to Newport Harbor in 1815, it seemed certain that the U.S. Navy was going to change. Peacetime meant that life would become routine

---

Above: John Bevan Irwin painted this 1815 depiction of the arrival of Commodore Stephen Decatur's squadron in Algiers. Decatur successfully negotiated a treaty with the Algerians.

and the chance of advancement and promotion would become slim. Many young officers, Perry among them, took this opportunity to apply for a furlough and to search for a new career. After moving to New York with his wife, Jane, Perry continued his former career on the high seas commanding merchant vessels. He missed the navy, however, and, after three years, Perry ended his furlough and returned to active duty. Perry was now twenty-four years old and the father of a baby girl named Sarah. His career, however, was uncertain, because it was more difficult to be promoted through the ranks during peacetime.

3. West Africa and the Caribbean

Upon his return to active duty, Matthew Calbraith Perry discovered that life in the U.S. Navy was different from what it had been only a few years before. There were no more wars with England or France, and the Barbary pirates of the Mediterranean coast had been subdued. For a young naval officer this meant that there were fewer chances to demonstrate bravery under fire. That made rapid promotion through the ranks difficult. Perry, however, chose to use this situation to demonstrate his talents as a leader and a diplomat. Perry's first assignment in the new U.S. Navy would take him to the coast of West Africa as part of a mission to take former slaves back to Africa.

The American Colonization Society was formed in 1816 in an attempt to address the issues of slavery and freedmen, as former slaves were called. The society proposed sending freedmen to establish a colony in Africa, and it worked to raise money for this cause. The society's members all felt that freedmen would be unable to assimilate into, or to fit in with, American society. Some members were abolitionists, a group of people who believed slavery was immoral. Other members were supporters of slavery. The abolitionists in the group believed that whites' prejudice against blacks would prevent assimilation. They hoped that repatriating the freedmen to Africa would allow them to live without racism and would bring a gradual end to slavery in the United States. Proslavery people, on the other hand, wanted to maintain the institution of slavery but to rid the country of free blacks, whom they saw as a threat to American society.

The slave trade had been illegal since 1808, but little had been done to enforce this law. In 1819, Congress declared that the African slave trade was piracy and authorized the navy to capture ships engaged in smuggling slaves into America.

On August 3, 1819, twenty-five-year-old Perry requested a position on the navy's corvette *Cyane*. The *Cyane*'s mission was to escort the *Elizabeth*, which would carry the first shipload of freedmen to Africa for the American Colonization Society's repatriation program. While waiting for the *Elizabeth* to gather supplies for the trip across the Atlantic and tools and building materials with which to establish the colony, Perry suffered personal tragedy as he learned of the untimely death of his oldest brother. On August 23, 1819, Oliver Hazard Perry, only thirty-four years old, had died from yellow fever. As a tribute to his brother, Perry

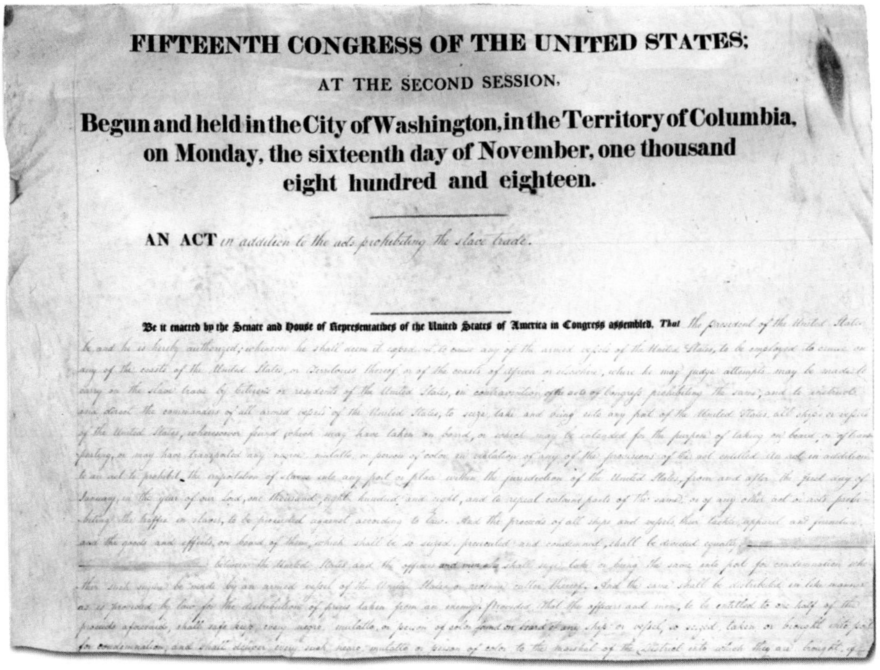

FIFTEENTH CONGRESS OF THE UNITED STATES;

AT THE SECOND SESSION,

Begun and held in the City of Washington, in the Territory of Columbia, on Monday, the sixteenth day of November, one thousand eight hundred and eighteen.

AN ACT in addition to the acts prohibiting the slave trade.

Be it enacted by the Senate and House of Representatives of the United States of America in Congress assembled, That the President of the United States be and he is hereby authorized, whenever he shall deem it expedient, to cause any of the armed vessels of the United States, to be employed to cruise on any of the coasts of the United States, or Territories thereof, or of the coasts of Africa or elsewhere, where he may judge attempts may be made to carry on the slave trade by citizens or residents of the United States, in contravention of the acts of Congress prohibiting the same, and to instruct and direct the commanders of all armed vessels of the United States, to seize, take and bring into any port of the United States, all ships or vessels of the United States, wheresoever found which may have taken on board, or which may be intended for the purpose of taking on board, or of transporting, or may have transported any negro, mulatto, or person of color in violation of any of the provisions of the act entitled An act in addition to an act to prohibit the importation of slaves into any port or place within the jurisdiction of the United States, from and after the first day of January, in the year of our Lord, one thousand, eight hundred and eight, and to repeal certain parts of the same, or of any other act or acts prohibiting the traffic in slaves, to be proceeded against according to law. And the proceeds of all ships and vessels, their tackle, apparel and furniture, and the goods and effects, on board of them, which shall be so seized, prosecuted and condemned, shall be divided equally between the United States and the officers and men who shall seize, take or bring the same into port for condemnation whether such seizure be made by an armed vessel of the United States or revenue cutter thereof. And the same shall be distributed in like manner as is provided by law for the distribution of prizes taken from an enemy: Provided, That the officers and men, to be entitled to one half of the proceeds aforesaid, shall safe keep every negro, mulatto, or person of color found on board of any ship or vessel, so seized, taken or brought into port for condemnation, and shall deliver every such negro, mulatto or person of color to the marshal of the District into which they are brought, ...

This 1819 Congressional act broadened the U.S. Navy's authority to stop ships suspected of carrying slaves. During the time that the *Cyane* escorted the *Elizabeth* to Africa, Perry and his men were able to capture several slave ships.

named his next child, a little girl born two months later, Jane Oliver Hazard Perry.

Finally, in February 1820, the *Elizabeth* was ready to set sail with the *Cyane* as its escort. As the ships neared the African coast in March 1820, Perry noted in his sea journal that Africa and its coast were generally unhealthy places to be stationed. He believed that every precaution should be taken to ensure the health and well-being of the crew. At the time, doctors and scientists believed that diseases such as yellow fever and "African fever," or malaria, were spread by harmful vapors called miasmas that were found in unhealthy places. Perry believed that the best way to keep his men healthy was to limit their time on shore, to avoid swampy areas and heavy work in the hot African sun, and to have the men stay as clean, cool, and dry as possible. Perry became famous within the navy for strictly enforcing health regulations such as these. On this trip, he was able to convince the ship's commanding officer, Captain Trenchard, to follow his ideas. Although neither man knew it at the time, Perry's prescription for disease prevention made good sense. It kept his men away from mosquitoes, which are the real cause of yellow fever.

The *Elizabeth* reached the African coast before the *Cyane* and then sailed westward to the British colony of Sierra Leone. The governor of Sierra Leone refused to let the colonists come ashore and sent them to Sherbro Island, a swampy, disease-infested island off the Sierra Leone coast. No one in the American Colonization Society ever thought that African Americans would not be welcomed by the native population or by their colonial overlords. It was the rainy season and the colonists were unprepared for life in this different and unfamiliar place. The colonists had been born and raised in the United States and were not used to the tropical climate. On March 27, 1820, the *Cyane* reached Cape Mesurado and then sailed to Sherbro Island and tried to offer the colonists some assistance. Shortly after arriving at the island, Captain Trenchard sailed back toward Cape

Mesurado to find a better location on the African mainland for the colonists to settle. The *Cyane* encountered a group of seven ships suspected of being slavers. After a quick chase, the *Cyane* captured all seven. A few days later, the *Cyane* captured two more suspected slave ships. All of the ships had illegal cargoes of slaves. Trenchard freed the human cargo and brought them to Sierra Leone.

On April 13, the *Cyane* arrived back at Cape Mesurado. Perry noted that this was the perfect place for the colonists to settle. According to his journal entry, the local population was friendly and the land was fertile. There was also a good harbor, and the constant sea breeze was considered to be the best way of preventing disease. After getting permission from the locals to settle, some of the colonists left Sherbro Island and established a new community, which they named Monrovia for President James Monroe. In 1824, the Monrovia settlement would be established as the capital of the colony of Liberia. The settlers who remained on Sherbro Island were less successful. All eighty-eight men, women, and children contracted malaria. By the end of the year, twenty-three had died and thirty-five others had either left for Sierra Leone or had returned to the United States. Only thirty of the settlers remained on Sherbro Island. The settlers who

---

Opposite: Perry's travels with the American Colonization Society took him to the British colony of Sierra Leone (*purple*), Sherbro Island (*blue*), and Cape Mesurado (*black*), where the Monrovia settlement was established in 1820. By the 1840s, this settlement became the colony of Liberia. Monrovia is now the name of the capital of Liberia.

moved to Monrovia fared better and the hope of a successful African American colony would keep Perry involved with the project through the years.

After more than ten months charting the waters off Africa's western coast, the *Cyane* returned to New York Harbor on December 25, 1820. This was a long, hard journey, yet Captain Trenchard, Perry, and the crew had fulfilled their mission. Patrolling the coast of Africa, they captured numerous slave ships and freed hundreds of captive slaves on African soil.

Perry spent the first six months of 1821 on extended leave in New York with his wife, Jane, and his four

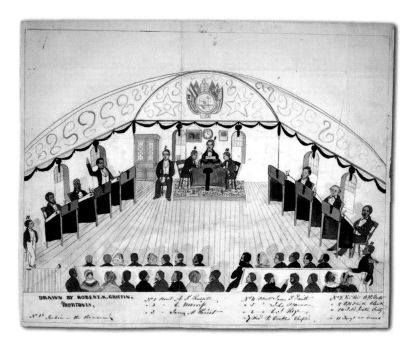

Liberia became an independent republic in 1847, after many difficulties in being established as a colony. Its constitution was based on the U.S. Constitution. Robert K. Griffin, an African American immigrant to Liberia, made this watercolor of Liberia's senate in 1856.

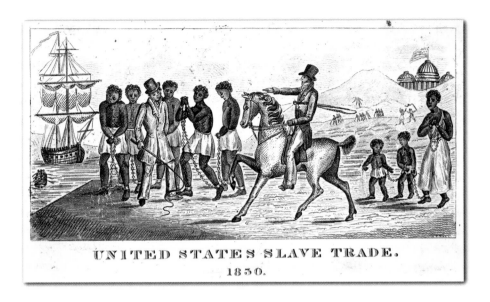

UNITED STATES SLAVE TRADE.
1830.

This abolitionist print from 1830 depicts the horrors of the slave trade. Slaves are chained together and are being sold. The American Colonization Society hoped to improve the lives of former slaves by establishing a colony in Africa. While some abolitionists were members of this society, they further hoped to bring about an end to slavery.

children. During the spring, at age twenty-seven, he was promoted to the rank of lieutenant commander and was given his first command, the *Shark*. Perry's orders were to bring Reverend Eli Ayers, the new U.S. commissioner of Liberia, to the Monrovia settlement.

Perry's style as commander of the *Shark* was based on his experiences serving under Commodore Rodgers. Relying on what later would be called the Rodgers system, Perry was a strict captain. Under his command, Perry tried to keep his men healthy and working hard. Although it was not a happy ship, the *Shark* was a healthy one. In addition to the measures he had taken to curb disease on his previous voyage to Africa, Perry also focused on the crew's diet. He insisted that the crew have supplies of fresh meat, vegetables, fruit, and water. Although doctors at the time did not know that diseases like scurvy were caused by vitamin deficiencies, they understood that a proper diet was important to the health of a ship's crew. Although some men resented Perry, they also recognized that it was because of his strict rules that they remained healthy. Not a single man on Perry's ship died from yellow fever or malaria.

While traveling to Monrovia, the *Shark* ran down several different ships suspected of being slavers, but few were. Of those that were slavers, none were owned or operated by Americans, so Perry did not have the authority to release the slaves or to take the crew members into custody.

After a brief winter break, in February 1822, the *Shark* ventured into Caribbean waters to search for pirates. Perry's orders sent him first to the Florida Keys, where he was to take formal possession of Key West under the terms of the Adams-Onís Treaty of 1819. In this treaty, the United States and Spain settled their claims in North America. Spain ceded Florida to the United States in exchange for the United States recognizing Spain's sovereignty over the Texas territory. A number of key officials in the U.S. Navy, Perry included, believed that Key West and the Florida Keys would be strategically valuable for commerce and American national security. Key West had a natural harbor and

J. Evans painted this watercolor of the schooner the *Shark*. Schooners were developed in North America in the eighteenth century by British colonists. They were developed to handle the changeable winds of coastal waters.

could serve as a place for ships to get provisions while sailing between the American mainland and the Caribbean. The Florida Keys could also be America's first point of defense against a foreign invasion.

After raising the American flag over Key West, the *Shark* began its search for pirates in the Caribbean, with little luck. Naval vessels in general were ill suited for chasing and capturing the smaller pirate ships. Pirates could navigate their ships in shallow waters and rivers, where ships like the *Shark* would run aground.

By early August 1822, heat and disease had taken their toll on Perry's crew, despite his strict health regime, and the West Indies Squadron left the Caribbean. The West Indies refers to the area between southeastern North America and northern South America, bordering on the Caribbean. After receiving provisions in Key West, Perry again sailed for the West African coast and Monrovia to search for slavers. He was pleased with what he saw during his brief stay at the African American colony and this only served to strengthen his belief in the correctness of the American Colonization Society's plan. As the *Shark* sailed back to the United States, it stopped and searched a number of suspected slavers on the return voyage. None of these

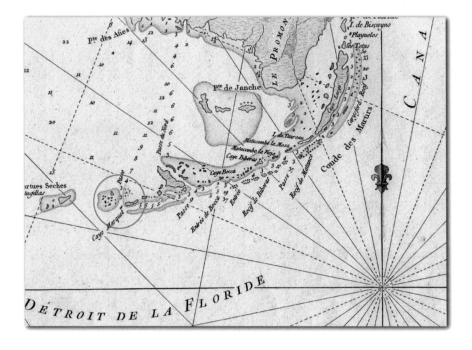

Key West (*blue circle*) is located off the coast of Florida. After the United States took possession of Florida, Key West quickly became a strategically located naval base. It was used for supplying ships on their way to the West Indies, and for policing pirate activity in the region.

ships flew the American flag, so Perry again concluded, wrongly, that Americans were not participating in the slave trade. In fact, American slavers carried false papers and flew French and Portuguese flags so that they would not be captured by American naval ships.

Perry's first command demonstrated that he was a capable officer. He played a major role in helping to establish the African American colony of Liberia and he worked tirelessly to police and suppress the slave trade. In the Caribbean, Perry learned of the frustrations of pirate hunting. Throughout the *Shark's* voyages, Perry insisted that his health regulations be closely followed. When the *Shark* returned to New York Harbor in December 1822, not a single crewman had died from disease. A strict disciplinarian, Perry was always serious and many crew members found him intimidating. His crew gave him the nickname Old Bruin, because of the way he barked out orders in a deep and powerful voice.

4. A Reformer on Land and at Sea

Matthew Calbraith Perry returned to New York in July 1823 and spent one year on shore duty at the Brooklyn Navy Yard. The previous year had taken its toll on his health. He was able to rest and spend some much-needed time with his wife and family. Perry was ready to return to sea in July 1824. He was ordered to join the ship *North Carolina*, which was bound for the Mediterranean Sea. Perry was first lieutenant, or second in command, on one of the navy's largest battleships. An added benefit of joining the *North Carolina* was that the Mediterranean Squadron was commanded by Commodore John Rodgers, Perry's mentor and former commander.

The Mediterranean Squadron had been sent to establish a greater American presence in the Mediterranean region and to protect commercial shipping interests against the increased pirate activity in the region. President John Quincy Adams also wanted Rodgers to establish a friendly dialogue with Greek and Turkish naval officials to strengthen diplomatic ties.

Another part of Rodgers's assignment was to restore discipline to the Mediterranean Squadron. Over the years, the seamen on the squadron had earned a reputation for being troublemakers.

As second in command, Perry was responsible for day-to-day operations of the *North Carolina*. He was in charge of the entire crew, including midshipmen and other officers. Perry was concerned with discipline, as was his mentor Commodore Rodgers. Regulations were to be followed. Orders were to be followed and executed in a "prompt, cheerful" manner, with no exceptions. Sailors who broke the rules were punished quickly and fairly. Perry believed also in preventing disciplinary problems.

Perry's promotion to first lieutenant of the Mediterranean Squadron reunited him with his mentor, Commodore Rodgers. Perry participated in the diplomatic goals of this mission. This 1816 engraving shows a previous Mediterranean squadron's return to the United States, sailing in a formation similar to that of the 1824–1827 Mediterranean Squadron.

If every sailor had a job, he would not only stay busy but also would have a sense of purpose.

Perry did his best to ensure that every man followed orders and behaved in a manner appropriate to his rank and position in the U.S. Navy. Officers were not only responsible for their crew's behavior, but also for the crew's health and morale. Not everyone appreciated Lieutenant Perry's attempts to restore order to the Mediterranean Squadron. On the *North Carolina*, Perry was seen as "a capable, energetic, and even zealous officer who won the respect, but not the admiration or affection, of the crew."

Rodgers's Mediterranean Squadron returned to the United States in July 1827, after more than two years at sea. Perry, then thirty-three years old, was sent to the Boston Navy Yard where he assumed command of the facility under Commodore Charles Morris. There he was responsible for naval recruitment, the construction of new shore facilities, and the repair of warships. Perry became an advocate for changes to the navy that he thought would strengthen national security and his branch of the service.

Perry believed that there were too few officers for efficient command. He proposed that the navy promote one hundred midshipmen to officer status and recruit four hundred new midshipmen. All sailors, especially the officers, needed better training. Perry thought that the ideal site for such a school was in Annapolis, along the shores of the Chesapeake Bay in Maryland. The secluded site was near the water, so students could receive practical shipboard training. The Naval School was later founded in 1845 without congressional funding. In 1850, the Naval School was renamed the United States Naval Academy. It later became known as Annapolis, for the town in which it is located.

Perry also argued in favor of an apprenticeship system in which teenage boys could enlist in and be trained by the navy. That way the navy would have a steady supply of able-bodied seamen and potential officers.

NAVAL ACADEMY AT ANNAPOLIS, MARYLAND.

W. R. Miller created this engraving of the U.S. Naval Academy around 1855. Former Secretary of the Navy George Bancroft founded the academy as the Naval School in 1845.

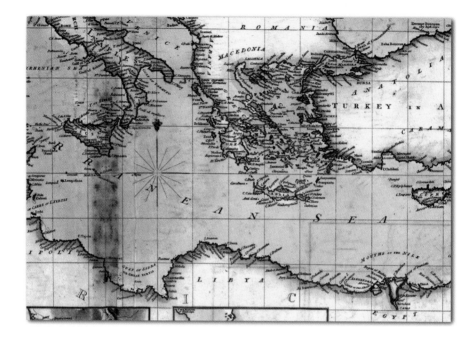

This 1817 hand-colored map of the Mediterranean Sea shows the areas of Europe and North Africa to which Perry traveled as part of the Mediterranean Squadron. The places he visited include Greece (*yellow*), Africa (*green*), and The Kingdom of the Two Sicilies (*orange*).

Finally, Perry proposed expanding the number of ranks as a way to improve organization and efficiency. Under the system of that time, there were three ranks: lieutenant, master commandant, and captain. The rank of commodore was honorary and given to officers who commanded a multiship station, such as a navy yard. Under Perry's proposal the honorary rank of commodore would become a formal rank and two new higher ranks, vice admiral and rear admiral, would be added. In this system, there would be one vice admiral, two rear admirals, six commodores, and a number of captains and lieutenants proportional to the number and size of ships. Perry's organizational proposal made sense to the navy but the plan failed in Congress.

By 1830, Perry had once again tired of shore duty. Although he enjoyed family life, he had become rather bored with his job of dealing with new recruits, supervising construction details, and entertaining the never-ending stream of officials who visited the Boston station. When approached to command the newly constructed sloop *Concord*, Perry gladly accepted. He was to bring the new U.S. minister to Russia, John Randolf, to Kronstadt on Kotlin Island in the Gulf of Finland about 18 miles (29 km) northwest of St. Petersburg, Russia. He was then to join the Mediterranean Squadron. It was common practice in the nineteenth century for warships to transport diplomats to their new posts.

After Randolf disembarked from the *Concord* at Kronstadt, Perry was able to continue with his official duties. He sailed through the Mediterranean visiting port cities and making a show of American naval power. American commerce in the Mediterranean had grown significantly and so had the threat to American ships. Perry believed that a show of force would discourage would-be pirates. In addition Perry made a number of diplomatic trips that included entertaining a Greek admiral and the khedive of Egypt.

During the summer and the autumn of 1832, Perry again learned the value of a gradual buildup of naval power as a way to reinforce the American position during negotiations. Ever since the Napoleonic Wars, there had been unresolved diplomatic issues with the Kingdom of the Two Sicilies, today part of Italy, involving the failure to pay a debt incurred for damage to American shipping vessels. Notified that negotiations had broken down, Perry sailed as part of a larger fleet into the Bay of Naples, off the coast of Italy. With an ever-growing American military presence in the bay, on October 14, 1832, Prince Cassaro, minister of foreign affairs, agreed to pay the United States 2,100,000 ducats, or $4,800,000. With the treaty signed, Perry set sail for home.

Arriving in New York in January 1833, Perry applied for and was granted command of the naval station in that city. He was now the commander of the naval rendezvous, known today as captain of the yard. For eight years Perry would serve in this fulfilling position.

As the commander of the navy yard, Perry could use his influence to put his ideas about naval reform into practice. In an article published in *Naval Magazine*, Perry took stock of the condition of the U.S. Navy and noted that it was eighth-largest in the world. Compared to England's and France's navy, the U.S. Navy was terribly out of date. Perry once again proposed adding new ranks to the three that existed and also recommended a system of promotion that was based on merit and service. Perry also argued once again that the navy should

Perry's "Thoughts on the Navy" article appeared in the January 1837 *Naval Magazine*. The article brought together ideas Perry had advocated throughout his career, and proposed changes he believed would make the U.S. Navy equal to European navies. These changes included adopting modern steam ships in place of traditional sailing vessels.

create an apprenticeship system that would train boys on merchant vessels. This was the only one of Perry's recommendations that succeeded. It would take years before his system was put into practice, however, and even then Perry's opponents would take every opportunity to criticize the program.

Perhaps Perry's most important contributions to the navy at this point in his career were views that earned him the name Father of the Steam Navy. Perry had long been familiar with steamships. He had watched the *Fulton*'s launch in 1814 and had seen the steam galliot *Sea Gull* chase pirates in the shallow

S. McElroy created this lithograph of the *Fulton II* around 1838. This steamer was intended for the defense of the New York harbor, not for duties that would take it to the open sea. The *Fulton II* cruised the Atlantic coast until it was decommissioned in 1842.

waters of the Caribbean. Perry believed that these new warships were the way of the future. His view was contrary to that of many in the navy.

Traditionalists opposed the use of steam power in warships for a number of reasons. Early steam engines were unreliable. They burned large quantities of coal, which took up valuable space and limited the cruising distance of the vessel. Early steamships had large, side-mounted paddle wheels, which were easy targets. Their deck-mounted engines were also easily disabled by a single, well-placed shot. This meant that steamships were vulnerable in battle. Many naval officers argued that steam-powered warships were ugly and dirty. They further argued that although it was an improvement that steamships could be steered against the wind and the current, less skill was required of the captain.

Perry had his chance to demonstrate the worthiness of steam power with the launching of the *Fulton II* in 1837. After supervising its construction in the New York Navy Yard, Perry was chosen to command the vessel. He was the perfect choice because he "held traditional views" about the navy but also was "one of the handful of American officers prepared to embrace new technology."

The *Fulton II*'s maiden voyage was not without problems. Its engines were too powerful for the paddle wheel, and coal consumption was high. After fixing these problems, Perry headed out to sea for a cruise along the East Coast. In May 1838, Perry steamed into the Washington,

D.C., harbor where he invited President Van Buren, members of his cabinet, and other important people aboard to inspect the ship. He gave them a firsthand demonstration of the ease with which a steamer could move against the current. Perhaps more than anything else, this trip to Washington, D.C., "helped advance the cause of steam power in the capital." Within one year, Congress approved funding for the construction of three additional steam-powered warships.

Because of this success, Perry also saw the need for a new steam corps. Steamships required mechanical and engineering skills which meant that people needed specialized training to serve on the steamships. The Navy Board of Commissioners approved Perry's recommendations, including positions for engineers, assistant engineers, firemen, and coal heavers. The board also approved newly designed uniforms and a special training program for engineers and firemen. Perry saw this as a perfect opportunity to show the effectiveness of his apprenticeship system. In 1838, Perry recruited the first group of apprentices. Apprentices received training in their specific area plus English composition, seamanship, and the traditional arts of war. The program worked well, and within five months Perry requested another twenty boys for enrollment in his program.

Having gained support in Washington and demonstrated the success of his apprenticeship program, Perry was sent to Britain and to France in June 1838 to collect information on steam warships in those countries, where the idea of a steam navy was gaining popularity. Perry returned in January 1839 even more convinced of the necessity of converting the U.S. Navy from sail to steam.

In June 1841, Perry took full command of the New York Navy Yard. He was given the honorary title of commodore, which meant that he was in command of everything from the ship-building and repair facilities to the recruiting offices and the ships

Abel P. Upshur (1790–1844) was secretary of the navy from 1841 to 1843. A.G. Heaton created this oil-on-canvas painting of Upshur in 1892.

that sailed in and out of the yard. That same year President John Tyler appointed his friend Abel P. Upshur to the position of secretary of the navy. Although he had no naval experience, Upshur relied on reform-minded officers for advice and followed many of their suggestions to improve and modernize the navy.

Perry continued to petition the new administration for improvements for the navy. Upshur was responsive to Perry's suggestions. Upshur wanted to redefine the navy's peacetime role through increased overseas commercial activity. Upshur recommended that the navy be transformed "from a small, defensive force of sailing ships into a large, modern steam navy." Upshur also envisioned organizational changes. As if reading from Perry's earlier letters, Upshur advocated changing the system of officer ranks, creating a naval academy, and instituting an apprenticeship system. Some of Upshur's recommendations were accepted and some were modified. Congress refused to support a naval academy, reduced the navy's budget, and rejected the creation of the rank of admiral. However, the changes that were made were good for the navy and Perry finally felt a sense of accomplishment for all of his reform efforts.

In the summer of 1842, Perry oversaw the construction of what would be one of the navy's last pure sailing vessels, the brig *Somers*. Perry wanted to demonstrate his apprenticeship system, so he had the *Somers* assigned as an experimental school ship under his direct supervision. Though Perry tried to select the ideal crew, there were some problems on board. Some members of the crew plotted a mutiny. This forced the commander of the ship, Master Commandant Alexander Slidell Mackenzie, Perry's brother-in-law and friend, to make a decision. After an investigation and court-martial proceedings at sea, the three leaders of the mutiny were sentenced to death. The *Somers* was at least one week out from the nearest port. To discourage other potential mutineers and to set an example, Mackenzie decided to carry out the execution on the ship. On December 1, the mutineers were hanged. The rest of the cruise went without further incident. After a brief stop in the Caribbean, the *Somers* arrived in New York on December 14, 1842.

Secretary of War John Spencer, the father of one of the men executed, demanded that Mackenzie be charged with his son's murder in a civilian court. In the end Mackenzie was acquitted of all charges, but Perry's apprenticeship system was dealt a major setback by the mutiny and its aftermath. There would not be another experimental training cruise for another twenty years.

5. Commodore of the Africa Squadron

The wake of the *Somers* mutiny was an upsetting time for Matthew Calbraith Perry. Although he was not personally criticized, the attacks on his colleagues and friends upset him greatly. Secretary of the Navy Upshur still had faith in Perry and appointed him commodore of the Africa Squadron in February 1843.

Perry's missions were to protect American trade and to police the slave trade. Commodore Perry set sail for the west coast of Africa on the *Saratoga* in June 1843. As always, Perry instructed his officers to enforce strict health regulations on their ships. Despite much complaining, Perry's squadron would suffer less from disease than did any other.

Perry was pleased to get command of the Africa Squadron. He wanted to return to West Africa to see the progress made by the African American settlements. Since his first mission with the American Colonization Society in 1820, the colonies had changed politically and economically. A number of new colonies had been established by other colonization societies.

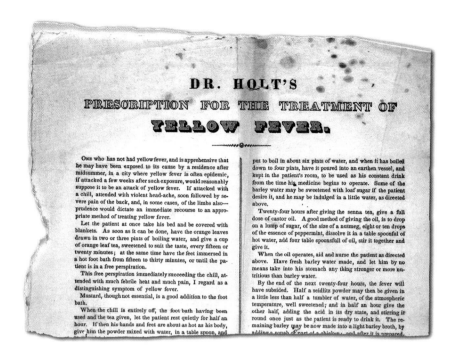

DR. HOLT'S

PRESCRIPTION FOR THE TREATMENT OF

YELLOW FEVER.

ONE who has not had yellow fever, and is apprehensive that he may have been exposed to its cause by a residence after midsummer, in a city where yellow fever is often epidemic, if attacked a few weeks after such exposure, would reasonably suppose it to be an attack of yellow fever. If attacked with a chill, attended with violent head-ache, soon followed by severe pain of the back, and, in some cases, of the limbs also—prudence would dictate an immediate recourse to an appropriate method of treating yellow fever.

Let the patient at once take his bed and be covered with blankets. As soon as it can be done, have the orange leaves drawn in two or three pints of boiling water, and give a cup of orange leaf tea, sweetened to suit the taste, every fifteen or twenty minutes; at the same time have the feet immersed in a hot foot bath from fifteen to thirty minutes, or until the patient is in a free perspiration.

This free perspiration immediately succeeding the chill, attended with much febrile heat and much pain, I regard as a distinguishing symptom of yellow fever.

Mustard, though not essential, is a good addition to the foot bath.

When the chill is entirely off, the foot bath having been used and the tea given, let the patient rest quietly for half an hour. If then his hands and feet are about as hot as his body, give him the powder mixed with water, in a table spoon, and put to boil in about six pints of water, and when it has boiled down to four pints, have it poured into an earthen vessel, and kept in the patient's room, to be used as his constant drink from the time his medicine begins to operate. Some of the barley water may be sweetened with loaf sugar if the patient desire it, and he may be indulged in a little water, as directed above.

Twenty-four hours after giving the senna tea, give a full dose of castor oil. A good method of giving the oil, is to drop on a lump of sugar, of the size of a nutmeg, eight or ten drops of the essence of peppermint, dissolve it in a table spoonful of hot water, add four table spoonsfull of oil, stir it together and give it.

When the oil operates, aid and nurse the patient as directed above. Have fresh barley water made, and let him by no means take into his stomach any thing stronger or more nutritious than barley water.

By the end of the next twenty-four hours, the fever will have subsided. Half a seidlitz powder may then be given in a little less than half a tumbler of water, of the atmospheric temperature, well sweetened; and in half an hour give the other half, adding the acid in its dry state, and stirring it round once just as the patient is ready to drink it. The remaining barley may be now made into a light barley broth, by adding a small part of a chicken, and after it is prepared,

In 1843, Dr. Holt of New Orleans wrote instructions for treating the symptoms of yellow fever. In it he advises patients to drink plenty of liquids, including water, herbal teas, and castor oil. Yellow fever continues to be a problem in warm climates. A vaccine was created in the 1930s to protect people from the disease. Until that time, many treatments had been tried.

There was also competition between the West African tribes and the African American settlements. Hostilities initially erupted over trade issues because the colonists interfered in the Africans' trade networks. There were also tensions over land. In Africa there was no such thing as private ownership of land and the tribes could not understand how they could be forbidden to enter what had always been communal land. Communal land is land that is open to everyone in a community. This led to a series of attacks by different African tribes on African American settlements and American ships.

Robert K. Griffin made this watercolor scene, entitled *Fish Town at Bassau, Liberia*, around 1856. The buildings in the background reveal the growing settlement of the young country.

Although Perry would have liked to get involved in protecting the settlements from tribal hostilities, protecting American merchant vessels was considered of greater importance. Perry learned of an incident at a village, Little Berebee, where the local tribe had attacked the schooner *Mary Carver* and murdered the captain and crew. For the next few weeks, the squadron moved down the coast and held conferences, known locally as palavers, with settlers and tribal councils. By moving with the full squadron and by making a grand entrance at each village, Perry hoped to give the appearance of a powerful American naval presence.

Arriving at Little Berebee on December 13, 1843, Perry learned that the attack on the *Mary Carver* had been unprovoked. Perry marched to a tent set up on the beach especially for the palaver, where he confronted the African leader King Ben Krako. Perry approached the king demanding an explanation for the incident. Using an interpreter, Krako replied that the ship's captain had killed two Africans and that his death was punishment for the crime. Believing the king to be lying, Perry uncharacteristically jumped to his feet and demanded a better explanation. In the growing tension, a shot was fired from outside the tent and mayhem erupted. King Krako tried to run, but Perry grabbed the king by his royal robe. The fight between the men continued until one of Perry's officers stabbed Krako.

When fighting had subsided, Perry ordered all Americans back to their ships. Eight Africans had died in the fight. King Krako died the following morning from his wounds. Perry was furious. He ordered Little Berebee burned, and, after consulting with his senior officers, ordered attacks on several other villages. Over the next three days, a group of American marines made examples of four African villages, all of which were burned. On the way back to Monrovia, Perry again used the threat of American naval force to ensure that local chiefs honored the agreements they had signed earlier with settlers and traders. Perry had done his job but was in an awkward position with tribal groups. If he was flexible with the tribal leaders, they would not respect their treaty obligations. If he was too forceful, tribal leaders would take out their anger on the settlers once the squadron was out of sight. Perry's strategy was to create goodwill, but also to scare the tribal leaders just enough that they would respect and fear American power. Neighboring chiefs were glad that Perry's men had killed King Krako, who they believed had been a violent and unfriendly man. The chiefs thought Perry had gone too far by ordering the burning of the four villages, though. The American government thought that Perry's actions had been justified and hoped that the Africans would not forget the violent dispute in future dealings with Americans.

Pleased that he had made Africa's shoreline and coastal waters safer for American commerce, Perry paid greater attention to the second part of his mission, which was to police the slave trade. With more than 2,500 miles (4,023 km) of coast to police, the Africa Squadron's four ships were overburdened. There were too few ships for too great an area. The navy's policy of "constant cruising," designed to have the squadron in as many places as possible, worked in the slavers' favor. They simply waited until the squadron passed, and then they went on with their illegal business. Many people in the navy and the government, including Commodore Perry, believed that the fact that American slave-trading vessels were not being captured meant

These modern watercolors show two American marines wearing uniforms like those worn by marines under Perry's command of the Africa Squadron. The private *(left)* carries a musket, while the first lieutenant *(right)* carries a special officer's sword called a Marmeluke sword.

that Americans were not involved in the slave trade. Unfortunately, this was not true.

Now on board the *Macedonian*, Perry made a final stop at Monrovia in September 1844. It would be the last time the commodore saw the coast of Africa. The journey home was uneventful. Perry looked forward to seeing his wife and family again. He had been at sea for two years and, despite all precautions, service in African waters had run him down and taken its toll on his health. As the *Macedonian* sailed into New York Harbor on April 28, 1845, the threat of war with Mexico loomed on the horizon. Commodore Perry would be back to sea in the not-too-distant future.

6. Commodore Perry of the Gulf Squadron

By the mid-1840s, tension between the United States and Mexico had been escalating for some time. One major factor in this tension was the movement of American settlers into western territories that belonged to Mexico. Then, in 1845, the United States annexed the territory of Texas from Mexico. In response, Mexico cut off its relations with the United States. The two countries further disputed whether this territory ended at the Nueces River, as Mexico claimed, or at the Rio Grande, as the United States claimed. In September 1845, President James K. Polk sent Congressman John Slidell to Mexico City on a diplomatic mission. His duties were to resolve the dispute over Texas and to arrange the purchase of the territories of New Mexico and California. Mexican officials were angered when they heard of the latter intention, which they saw as breaking up their young country, and they refused to meet with Slidell. Upon learning of this refusal, Polk sent troops to occupy the area between the Nueces River and the Rio Grande. On May 9, 1846,

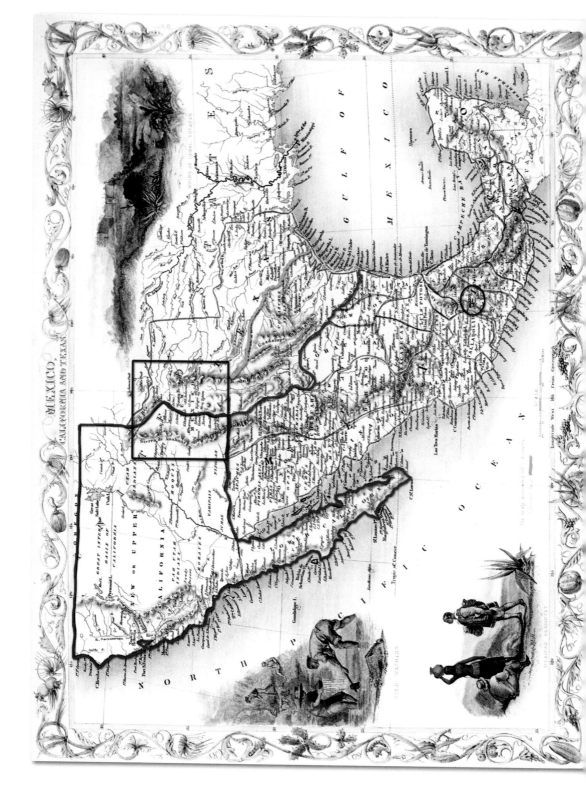

President Polk was informed that Mexican troops had attacked these forces on April 25. On May 13, Congress declared war on Mexico.

This would be a different kind of war for the U.S. Navy. Unlike its major part in the War of 1812, the navy's role in this conflict would be a supporting one. War planners decided that the navy should support ground forces by capturing small ports, establishing a coastal blockade, and protecting supply routes. There were no plans for a major sea offensive because Mexico did not have a large navy.

Matthew Calbraith Perry was on shore duty when Secretary of the Navy George Bancroft asked him if he would be interested in commanding the Gulf Squadron. Perry was to take over for Commodore David Connor, who, although in poor health, refused to give up command.

In September 1846, with the war only four months old, Perry was surprised to find morale so low in the Gulf Squadron. The Gulf Squadron was ordered to blockade the coast, which was considered a boring duty. To make matters worse, it was the rainy season, and the rain brought mosquitoes, which brought yellow fever and malaria. Navigation was also a problem.

Opposite: This 1845 map shows the United States and Mexico along with the Nueces River (*yellow*) and the Rio Grande (*dark red*), which were the rivers that marked the two disputed borders of the Texas territory (*red*). New Mexico (*blue*) and California (*green*) are two territories that the United States wished to purchase from Mexico. Mexico City (*black circle*) is the capital of Mexico.

There were few natural harbors and most inlets were blocked by sandbars, which made it impossible for large naval vessels to sail inland. Because of this, blockade cruising had to be done on small ships. The men of the Gulf Squadron viewed their hot, cramped, and unhealthy ships as prisons.

In October, Commodore Connor was attempting his second assault on the Mexican coastal town Alvarado. On the first try, his ships ran aground on a sandbar and he ordered his men to pull back. On the second try, another ship got stuck on a sandbar and once again Connor decided to withdraw. Even though he was right in his decision, Connor's action further depressed the squadron's morale.

At noon on October 23, 1846, the *Vixen* and the *McLane* moved toward the river that would take them to the province of Tabasco. The *Vixen* passed over a sandbar that blocked entry to the river with ease but the *McLane* ran aground. Without hesitating, Perry continued upriver. By 3:00 P.M., Perry had approached Frontera, the first town along the river, where his lookouts spotted two Mexican steamers. Perry ordered the *Vixen* to accelerate to full speed. Without firing a shot, Perry and his men captured the two steamers plus two schooners that were tied up at the riverfront port. Wasting no time, Perry sent marines to secure the town.

The American force continued to sail upriver for Tabasco the next morning. Perry's men were on constant

War News from Mexico by Richard Caton Woodville shows people gathered to read about the Mexican War. People were divided about the war. Many Democrats, especially those in the South, favored the war. Many Whigs felt that President Polk's reasons were wrong and that he intended to acquire land to expand slaveholding territory.

guard against potential ambush during the 70-mile (113-km) journey, because Mexican troops could hide in the dense jungle along the river. As they continued toward Tabasco, Perry's squadron captured six more enemy vessels.

Just after noon on the second day, lookouts on the *Vixen* spotted Tabasco. Perry moved the squadron into battle formation, anchored, and sent three officers ashore to demand the immediate surrender of the city. Don Juan Bautista Traconis, the Mexican general in command, refused to surrender and dared Perry to attack. Perry opened fire and ordered his marines to take the city. Before nightfall, in a hail of musket and cannon fire, the marines fought their way to the city plaza. That night, word came that the city elders wanted to surrender, but that Traconis refused to give up. Wanting to avoid further bloodshed, Perry decided to move his force downriver.

The next morning, Mexican troops opened fire. Perry again turned his artillery on the city and soon the Mexicans surrendered. Perry ordered a cease-fire and sent Captain Forrest to investigate. Forrest received a letter with the request that the squadron stop firing. Perry agreed and raised a flag of truce over the *Vixen*. As the squadron attempted to leave, one of the ships ran aground. Mexican soldiers opened fire on the ship and its crew. Angered at the unnecessary loss of life and of Traconis's breach of the truce, Perry turned his guns loose on the city. Thirty minutes later much of Tabasco lay in ruins. Amazingly there were only four civilian deaths.

Perry's squadron left Tabasco and rejoined the main squadron in the Gulf of Mexico without further incident. Although it was a minor skirmish with few casualties, the assault on Tabasco was important. While the city had not been surrendered, the squadron had captured nine enemy ships and had blocked trade through Tabasco. These successes raised the squadron's morale.

In December 1846, Connor ordered Perry to take Yucatán, a southern Mexican province. Perry's objectives were to capture the key port town of Laguna, to destroy public buildings, to clear foreign merchant ships from the area, and to set up a small force to patrol the coast. Accomplishing these goals turned out to be relatively easy. Perry's force entered Laguna's harbor on December 20. Local officials surrendered the next morning. Two days later, Perry's Laguna mission was accomplished. He left a detachment of marines to occupy Laguna's forts and two ships to patrol the harbor and coast. After rejoining the main squadron the following week, Connor ordered Perry to return to the Norfolk Navy Yard in Virginia and to oversee repairs on the steamer *Mississippi*.

Perry immediately set about having the *Mississippi* repaired. He brought the navy's chief engineer to Norfolk, where crews of mechanics worked nonstop to finish the job. Perry also met with the secretary of the navy and even with President Polk. Perry wanted to settle the issue of his command of the Gulf Squadron. Sixteen months had passed since he was offered command of the Gulf Squadron, but Connor had not stepped down. The president, realizing that a quick war was now out of the question, decided that he needed a healthy, strong officer to command the Gulf Squadron. On February 26, 1847, President Polk ordered Perry "to relieve Commodore Connor in the command of the Gulf Squadron."

General Winfield Scott (1786–1866) is shown in a detail from a Currier & Ives lithograph from around 1847. After his success as a general in the Mexican War, Scott ran as the Whig candidate for president in 1852, but he lost to Franklin Pierce.

Perry arrived back in the Gulf of Mexico on March 20, 1847, and relieved Connor of his command in the middle of the invasion of Veracruz, an important port city that, if captured, would give American forces a quick route to the Mexican capital, Mexico City. American forces under the combined command of Commodore Connor and General Winfield Scott had recently landed a force of 8,600

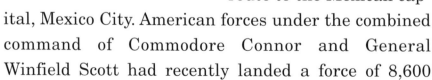

men. Perry met with Scott and Connor to discuss plans for the siege of Veracruz.

On March 22, 1847, General Scott began to bombard the city. Two days later American naval batteries opened fire. In forty-eight hours they fired more than one thousand shells and eight hundred rounds of shot. Scott was planning to launch a major assault on the city, but, just before he did, the Mexican army raised the white flag and surrendered.

Immediately after the fall of Veracruz, Scott and his troops began their march to Mexico City. The cities of Veracruz, Alvarado, and Tampico were under American control. Only four other key cities remained: Tuxpan, Coatzlcoalcos, Tabasco, and Laguna. Perry knew that he would need strong ground troops to take the cities. To do this, Perry created the navy's first infantry brigade. The navy infantry brigade, two thousand men strong, would drill and fight on land and at sea.

Perry assembled a flotilla of three steam warships, three bomb brigs, and a landing force of nearly one thousand five hundred men. American forces took Tuxpan, Coatzlcoalcos, and Laguna in quick succession. After careful planning, the second assault on Tabasco began on June 14, 1847. After entering the Grijalva River, the flotilla moved upriver for two days. On the third day, they encountered underwater obstacles designed to stop or sink enemy ships. At that point Perry decided to take Tabasco by land. Commander

Buchanan selected a site on which to land the assault force, and in less than ten minutes 1,100 men were ashore with Perry at the lead.

The force came under fire as it approached the town of Acachapan. Mexican forces, under the command of Colonel Hidalgo, were waiting for the American forces. Perry himself led the attack against Hidalgo. The sight of the Old Bruin, at age fifty-three, charging with sword in hand, was an inspiration to his men. Hidalgo's soldiers retreated toward Tabasco.

This is a detail from an 1847 engraving by navy lieutenant H. Walke. It depicts Perry's naval expedition in Mexico, at a place called the Devil's Bend, where the Grijalva River weaves through dense jungle. In the background the naval battleships can be seen forming the second assault on Tabasco in June 1847.

While Perry was leading the charge on Acachapan, the river flotilla was clearing the underwater obstacles in order to reopen the river to American warships. By the time the flotilla reached Acachapan, Perry's forces had begun their march toward Tabasco but had become bogged down in the swamps and the jungle along the way. It took the land forces several hours to reach Tabasco. When they arrived, they saw an American flag flying over the city. Much to their surprise, the defenders had already surrendered to the flotilla. The fall of Tabasco was a major victory for Perry and the U.S. Navy. Perry issued a general order thanking everyone involved.

Perry remained in Tabasco until mid-July 1847. The Mexican War ended in May 1848. Commodore Perry returned to New York in July exhausted but satisfied. He was now the navy's highest-ranking officer. He had clearly demonstrated his abilities as a soldier, commander, diplomat, and military planner. At that moment, he was looking forward to shore duty and to seeing his family again, but his reputation and abilities would again take him to new places.

7. The Opening of Japan

In the mid-nineteenth century, America was expanding westward. The Oregon Territory had been acquired in 1846. California had become a U.S. territory in 1848. People were moving to the Pacific coast in large numbers. At the same time, America's whaling fleet moved into the North Pacific, and, not long after, a trans-Pacific steamship line was completed.

Although he had served in the U.S. Navy for more than forty years, Matthew Calbraith Perry had never sailed in Pacific waters. After returning from the Mexican War, he developed a strong interest in Japan and Asia. He had heard stories about China and Japan from a number of relatives and friends. The Chinese trade had great economic potential, but Americans were not important players in this market. European countries such as Great Britain and the Netherlands had long dominated the East Indies trade. If the United States could take advantage of the Pacific route to Asia, they could soon establish a strong presence in the region. With his eye on Asia,

The East Indies Trade

The East Indies trade was established by the Portuguese in the 1550s as a way to avoid the merchants who controlled the overland trade routes between Europe and Asia. The Portuguese bought spices, such as pepper and nutmeg, that were valuable in Europe. With the founding of the Britain's East India Company in 1600 and Netherlands' Dutch East India Company in 1602, the British and the Dutch had replaced the Portuguese as the major European traders in Asia. The Dutch concentrated their efforts on the spice trade in Indonesia, then known as the East Indies. The British focused on the tea trade in India. China became an important port of call for American merchants during the nineteenth century. Many prominent New England merchant families were active in the China and East Indies trade. They traded things like rum and silver for Chinese tea and Indonesian spices.

Perry continued to promote a larger steam navy, but he knew firsthand the problems of supplying steam warships with coal. For the United States to be dominant in the Pacific Ocean, he argued, it would need coaling stations. Japan could be an important refueling stop for American ships on their way to China.

Most Americans knew little about Japan. Japan had been closed to Westerners since 1638. Before 1638, Westerners had been free to travel and to trade in Japan. Seeing the opportunity to convert the Japanese to Christianity, missionaries had gone to the island nation. They had some success, which led to problems with the government. The Tokugawa shoguns demanded total loyalty from every Japanese. The shoguns feared that, through Christianity, Western powers and influence would take over Japan. Although some of the reasons for closing Japan

This stone was erected on the Japanese island of Amakusa. It commemorates the deaths of more than 11,000 Japanese Christians who were put to death in 1637. The Christians had rebelled by refusing to pledge total loyalty Tokugawa shoguns.

Shogun rulers, as seen in this detail from a nineteenth-century woodblock print, were the leaders in a strict class system. The ranks in Tokugawa society were warriors, farmers, craftspeople, and merchants. Members of the warrior class, known as samurai, often worked as bureaucrats in towns.

remain a mystery, one major reason the Japanese government decided to close the country was a rebellion against the Tokugawa authority by Japanese Christians in 1637. The official policy then became to close out Christianity and outsiders, to reduce the likelihood of another rebellion, even if this seclusion meant the loss of trade. Except for a handful of Dutch traders who lived on a man-made island in Nagasaki Harbor, and regular visits by Chinese, Korean, and Southeast Asian merchant ships, Japan remained closed to the world and at peace for more than two hundred years. This period became known as the Tokugawa, or Edo, period in Japanese history.

A number of European countries had tried to reestablish relations with Japan without success. Between 1791 and 1807, the United States sent ten trade missions to Japan but each failed. During the 1840s, the U.S. government wanted more than ever to establish formal relations with Japan. A number of missions were sent, but each time the naval officer in charge failed to get the Japanese to agree to any changes.

In January 1851, Commodore Perry contacted Secretary of the Navy William Graham with a plan for an expedition to Japan. Because all previous attempts to establish trade relations with Japan had failed, Perry proposed that initial discussions focus on getting refuge and provisions for the whaling fleet. Rather than sailing into Nagasaki, where they would be expected, Perry suggested that a squadron arrive at another location, such as Uraga, which was closer to Edo, where Perry believed the emperor lived. Perry intended for the unexpected arrival to catch the Japanese off guard and impress them with America's naval power. In dealing directly with Japanese officials, who were known to be good negotiators, Perry recommended being patient but firm. For this task he said that only an experienced naval officer would do. Perry had no intention of undertaking

This detail from a Japanese scroll depicts a Japanese perspective of the arrival of Perry and the East India Squadron at Kurihama, Japan, in July 1853. The ship depicted is a navy steamer, possibly the USS *Susquehanna*.

this mission himself, though. In November 1851, Commodore Perry was informed that he was to assume command of the East India Squadron and undertake the Japanese mission. Perry considered this assignment a demotion. Perry wrote to Secretary of the Navy Graham to express his disappointment and requested that the squadron's mission be expanded to be more appropriate for someone of his position.

With a presidential election only months away, the Fillmore administration agreed with Perry. It would look good for the president if he could open Japan.

This American perspective of the arrival of the East India Squadron in Japan is a lithograph created by W. Heine in 1856. It depicts the ships *Mississippi*, *Susquehanna*, *Saratoga*, and *Plymouth* in Uraga Bay.

Perry insisted that the administration make this a major effort. Secretary Graham agreed to Perry's proposal and, by January 1852, the commodore was hard at work planning the Japan expedition. Graham worked to make sure that Perry had everything he needed, including the largest naval force ever sent overseas by the United States.

Bound for China, Commodore Perry left the Norfolk Naval Yard aboard the steamer *Mississippi* on November 24, 1852. The voyage went well, but the *Mississippi*'s constant need for coal reminded Perry of the importance of his mission. The *Mississippi* burned more than 2,337 tons (2,374.5 t) of coal on its journey from the United States to China.

On May 16, 1853, the *Mississippi* steamed out of Shanghai, China, toward Japan. After making several stops, Perry's squadron sailed toward Uraga Bay. Leaving one ship behind, the squadron consisted of the *Susquehanna*, the *Saratoga*, the *Mississippi*, and the *Plymouth*. Perry must have been nervous. Every person who had gone before him had failed to negotiate a treaty with Japan. Perry knew that he could force the Japanese to sign a treaty under the threat of war, but he hoped for friendly relations.

On July 8, 1853, Perry's squadron steamed into Uraga Bay. Each ship was fully prepared for action. Every cannon was loaded and ready to fire. Every officer and sailor stood ready with loaded firearms at his side. From the shore, the Japanese fired two cannon shots that warned of Perry's arrival, and guard boats carrying Japanese soldiers and officials came out to meet Perry's fleet. Farther inland in Edo, two hundred thousand samurai scrambled to arms in case of an invasion. The guard boats surrounded the American ships and attempted to board, but Perry's men would not allow any Japanese on board. After several tense minutes, one guard boat rowed up to the *Susquehanna* with a sign in French stating that the ships should leave immediately. Then a Japanese interpreter

An unknown Japanese photographer took this late-nineteenth-century photo of a samurai. The samurai is shown wearing his armor and weapons. Samurai carried two swords, which indicated their high-ranking, warrior status in Tokugawa society.

speaking in Dutch informed one of Perry's lieutenants that a high official was in the boat and that he wished to be received. Perry's interpreter replied that the official could not meet with the commodore because he was a personal representative of the president of the United States and would receive only the highest-ranking government officials. When the Japanese official in the boat claimed to be the vice governor of Uraga, he was allowed on board but was not permitted to speak with Commodore Perry. As it turned out, the Japanese official was Nakajima Saburonosuke, an aide to the vice governor, not the vice governor himself. Nakajima was only allowed to speak with Perry's flag lieutenant, John Contee.

Lieutenant Contee told Nakajima that Perry had come to deliver a letter to the emperor from the president of the United States. When Nakajima replied that all foreign ships and communications should be sent through the Dutch trade factory at Nagasaki, Contee politely refused, saying they had come to Uraga to be near Edo. Contee also told the Japanese aide that the guard boats surrounding Perry's squadron could either choose to leave or to be compelled to do so. Nakajima sent away most of the guard boats and then stated that he too would leave but would return the next day after having consulted with the governor. In the meantime, he offered Contee food, water, and fuel. Perry knew that this was a Japanese tactic that took away a foreign ship's excuse for remaining in Japanese waters. Already prepared with an answer by Perry, Contee again politely refused and instead offered to share the American's food with them. Speechless, Nakajima departed the *Susquehanna*.

Perry established a number of important principles through his first meeting with the Japanese. By refusing to meet with anyone other than a high official, Perry had made himself more exclusive and therefore more important in the eyes of the Japanese. By keeping guard boats away and refusing to allow Japanese soldiers access to his ship, Perry demonstrated that only officials were allowed on board and that only official business would be conducted on the flagship. These tactics gave Perry power over Nakajima, who was made to operate on Perry's terms.

That night Perry ordered his men to stay alert in case of a surprise attack. Later a brilliant orange and blue meteor streaked across the night sky. Lieutenant John Duer, commander of the *Mississippi*, recorded it as an omen of good fortune. He wrote in his journal that the meteor was a sign that Perry would bring together the people of America and Japan.

When the sun came up on the morning of July 9, it revealed a country more beautiful than anyone on board the *Susquehanna* had expected. To the west Mt. Fuji rose high above the deep green, pine-covered hills. Small boats moved throughout Uraga Bay, and a busy village could be seen along the coast. Soon a boat appeared and a man claiming to be the governor came aboard. He was Kayama Eizaemon, the governor's aide and the chief of police. Because Kayama was ranked higher than Nakajima, he was allowed to speak with Commanders Buchanan and Adams. Kayama repeated what had been said the night before. Buchanan and Adams knew Perry's orders well and no matter how many times Kayama restated his position, the two commanders refused to comply. Seeing that his attempts to move the squadron to Nagasaki were useless, Kayama stated that he would need to contact the government in Edo for further instructions, and that it would take at least eight days for an answer. Through his commanders, Perry replied that he would only wait three days before moving toward Edo.

Perry's actions had taken the Tokugawa government by surprise. When Perry arrived, Japan was in a state of political and social crisis. The government was divided over foreign policy. Some leaders thought that Japan should open a few more ports to foreign trade. Others insisted that things remain as they were and even argued that, if necessary, Japan should go to war. Officials realized that after more than two centuries of peace, Japan was not

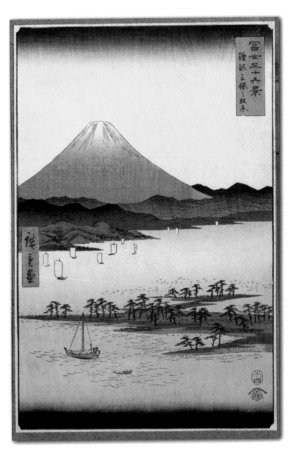

The famous Japanese artist Andō Hiroshige (1797–1858) created this woodblock print in 1853. This is a detail from a series of prints entitled *36 Views of Mt. Fuji*. Mt. Fuji is the largest mountain in Japan and is a popular theme in Japanese art.

technologically capable of fending off an invasion.

Not knowing what else to do, the Tokugawa government decided to stall and to try to keep Perry as far away from Edo as possible. The man responsible for Tokugawa policy, Abe Masahiro, sent word to Perry that the government would accept President Fillmore's letters at Uraga and an answer would be sent the following spring. During the time between accepting the letters and providing an answer, Abe planned on meeting with various officials to find a strategy for dealing with the Americans.

On July 12, Kayama returned to the *Susquehanna* with news that a high government official would accept President Fillmore's letters on shore at a ceremony held at the town of Kurihama, located a few miles (km) from Uraga. The Japanese government's reply, however, would come through either Dutch or Chinese middlemen at Nagasaki. Perry said that he would consider it an insult if the emperor of Japan could not deliver directly a letter to the president's representatives. He suggested that such insults might need to be avenged. Kayama left the *Susquehanna* but returned later that day to assure Perry that he would be received by an important official.

On the morning of July 14, 1853, the *Susquehanna* and the *Mississippi* steamed closer to Kurihama.

Opposite: This detail from an 1855 map of Japan shows the places visited by Perry and the East India Squadron: Yokohama; Kanagawa; and Edo, spelled Yedo here, and now called Tokyo *(top inset)*. Nagasaki *(bottom inset)* is where the Japanese wanted to send the squadron.

Perry and his senior officers had planned the landing with care, with cannons facing the beach in case of any trouble. To meet the Japanese delegation of officials and approximately five thousand soldiers, Perry brought two hundred fifty well-armed marines and sailors. After landing, Perry's men quickly formed into a procession and marched down the beach while the ship's band played the national anthem and "Hail Columbia." Perry presented President Fillmore's letters in an elaborate wooden box and the Japanese minister gave Perry a scroll acknowledging receipt of the president's letters and told the Americans that they could now leave. Perry noted that he would be back in the spring for a formal reply. When asked if he would be coming back with all four warships, Perry replied that he would bring that many and more. With that the ceremony was over.

Although he had been told to leave, Perry continued to steam around Uraga and Edo Bay. Perry wanted to show the Japanese how little their order meant to him. He believed that a showing of strong will would produce more favorable consideration of the president's letter. On July 16, Perry moved the squadron back to Uraga, at which point Kayama came aboard saying that he was sure that the president's letter would be well received. The squadron left Uraga Bay, proud of their success.

In February 1854, Perry was ready to return to Japan. As before, he had planned every detail. Returning with six more ships, Perry intended to make a show of American naval power once again. He intended to let Japanese officials know that America wanted friendly relations and that he would make reasonable demands, but that he would not back down. He also brought gifts for the Japanese, including a working quarter-scale railroad that would demonstrate American industrial power.

Gessan Ogata created this watercolor showing the initial ceremony at Kurihama in July 1853. In this initial meeting, Perry gave the Japanese minister a letter from President Fillmore. In return, the minister gave Perry a scroll confirming that he had received the letter. The two sides then made arrangements to meet the next spring.

When Commodore Perry saw Mt. Fuji again from the mouth of Edo Bay, it was a cold, windy morning. He worried that, during his seven-month absence from Japan, the Tokugawa government might have become better prepared to deal with his tactics. Just the opposite had happened. After his departure, Abe sent copies of President Fillmore's letters to various government officials and to the emperor, asking for their opinions on the best way to deal with the Americans. By asking the opinion of others in this matter of foreign policy, the Tokugawa government, led by the shogun in Edo, demonstrated its weakness. Three groups emerged with different solutions. One group recommended that Japan immediately strengthen its defenses so that they could reject American demands and go to war if necessary. Another believed that trade was a good thing and urged bargaining with Perry to avoid war. A third group opposed trade, but also knew that Japan could not win a war against the Americans. They told Abe only to avoid war.

Before negotiations could begin, Perry and the Japanese needed to agree on a location at which to hold them. The Japanese government refused to allow Perry to come to Edo, but Perry wanted to be as close as possible to the seat of government. After two weeks of negotiating, they agreed on a small fishing village, Yokohama, that stood between Uraga and Edo. The Japanese quickly built a large reception hall in Yokohama and set March 8 as the day to begin discussions.

On March 8, 1854, Perry and his men landed a short distance from the new building. Five hundred marines, sailors, and musicians, all armed and wearing full dress uniform, accompanied the commodore as he marched to the hall. A delegation of five Japanese commissioners greeted Perry. Communications were difficult. Perry's English was translated into Dutch, then a Japanese translator translated the Dutch into Japanese. For the Japanese the process went the other way. All of Perry's documents were written in English, Dutch, and Chinese, and the Japanese documents were written in Japanese, Dutch, and Chinese.

Councillor Hayashi Noburo opened negotiations by presenting an official written response to President Fillmore's letter. It mentioned the recent death of the shogun and apologized for not being able to change the laws of the land. In the spirit of cooperation, however, Japan would accept the following terms. Japan would give fresh food, water, and fuel to ships and sailors in trouble. Japan would also open a harbor to American ships in five years. In the meantime, coal could be purchased at Nagasaki. With this the Japanese announced that they were finished and would sign the treaty the next day.

Next spread: This hand-colored lithograph shows the squadron's arrival in March 1854 at the fishing village of Yokohama. The landing area was only a short distance from a reception hall that the Japanese had built specially for the occasion of negotiations with the United States.

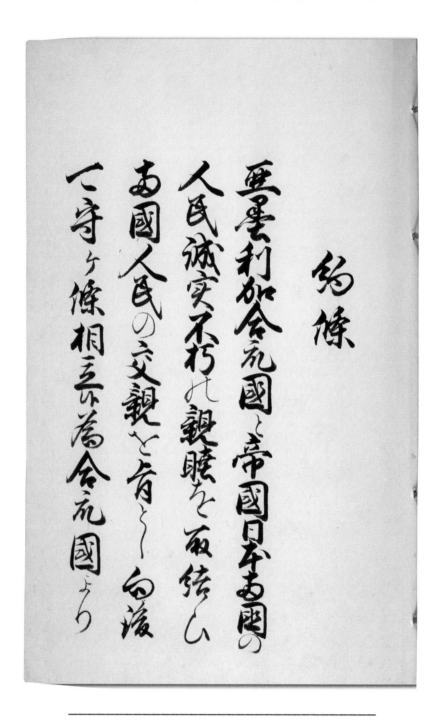

約條

亜墨利加合衆國と帝國日本両國の
人民誠実不朽ル親睦を取結ひ
あ國人民の交親と有と一白渡
一守ヶ條相立ニ爲合衆國より

The United States–Japan Treaty of Peace and Friendship, also known as the Treaty of Kanagawa, was signed March 31, 1854. The treaty opened up the possibility of trade relations between the two countries.

To Perry this must have been shocking. It had taken two weeks to settle disagreements on a meeting place, but, in a matter of minutes, the Japanese had given America everything President Fillmore wanted. Perry sensed he had the advantage and pressed for more. He wanted a treaty similar to the one the United States had with China, which included provisions for trade. Hayashi held firm. It took until March 31, 1854, for both sides to agree on all terms and for the documents to be translated into all the different languages. Despite the length of negotiations, the Treaty of Kanagawa, also known as the United States–Japan Treaty of Peace and Friendship, was a document that lived up to its name. As soon as the treaty was signed, relations between the Japanese and American negotiators warmed up. Although sometimes shocked at Japanese customs, Perry and his officers left Japan with a favorable impression of the country and its people. The Japanese were also impressed by the Americans. Once only thought of as "hairy barbarians," the Americans were now seen as friendly, good-natured people.

For Japan the Treaty of Kanagawa ended the country's two-hundred-year-old policy of national isolation. By the end of the next year there would be more treaties with more foreign powers, foreign trade, and consuls stationed in Yokohama. This also led to the final blow for the Tokugawa government. A revolution in 1868 would topple the Tokugawa and move Japan into the modern age.

For Perry, it was the crowning achievement of a long and successful naval career. He would return to China to serve out his term as commodore of the East India Squadron. On September 11, 1854, Commodore Perry boarded the steamer *Hindostan* for the long voyage home. His men lined the decks of the *Mississippi* and the *Macedonian* to honor their commodore with two thirteen-gun salutes. After forty-five years in the navy, this would be Perry's final command.

8. The Commodore's Final Days

When Matthew Calbraith Perry arrived home in January 1855, he was praised by businessmen and government officials. There were lavish dinners and receptions in his honor. He was given expensive gifts, and special medals were created to celebrate the event. Perry even received letters of congratulations from former president Millard Fillmore, the secretary of state, the secretary of the navy, and other high-ranking officials.

Public praise for Perry and the treaty was less significant. Although newspapers carried stories of the treaty, most people still knew little about Japan and paid scant attention to the news. Japan seemed like a small exotic island with little economic potential. Even before the official book describing the expedition was published in 1856, entitled *Narrative of the Expedition of an American Squadron to the China Seas and Japan*, two other accounts were published that criticized Perry for being arrogant and for failing to conclude a commercial treaty.

北亞墨利加人物

ペルリ像

This portrait of Perry was created around 1854. The title translates from the Japanese as *A North American Portrait of Perry*. It is a Japanese woodblock print, showing Perry in his naval uniform.

Rather than dwell on matters beyond his control, Commodore Perry got back to his work on naval reform. He served briefly on the Naval Retirement Board, a job that he particularly disliked. The board was designed to force old officers into retirement so that younger officers could move up in the ranks. Perry believed that it was illegal and purely political but served on it nonetheless. All the while, Perry

This bronze commemorative Perry medal is a modern restrike of the original, made around 1856, The front *(left)* shows Perry in profile, created from an 1856 daguerreotype. The reverse *(right)* describes Perry's achievements in the opening of Japan.

worked on the official narrative of the Japan expedition, composed of three volumes. The first volume was released during the spring of 1856. The second and third volumes followed one year later.

During this time, Perry thought about the United States' role in Asia and the Pacific. He believed that in the future Japan would serve an important role as a regional power and that the United States should establish a steamship line to connect the United States with China and Japan. He thought that the United States should establish settlements in the Pacific. Perry believed that the island of Formosa, now known as Taiwan, and the Bonin Islands, off the coast of Japan, would be good locations for American settlers because they could serve as coaling and supply stations for American ships. Perry viewed America's growth in trade in the East as a beneficial move, much like America's policy of expansion into Texas, California, and Oregon. Knowing that the government opposed establishing colonies, Perry argued that these Eastern settlements could be independent, and friendly to American commerce and government. His vision, although not well thought out, was of an "American commercial and maritime empire in East Asia."

Years of service on the high seas had taken their toll on Perry's health. Gradually, he had grown weaker and, by 1857, was spending more and more time in bed. In February 1858, Commodore Perry caught what appeared to be a severe cold and was confined to bed for several weeks. He received medical treatment, but his health continued to decline. On March 4, 1858, Commodore Perry died at age sixty-three. He was entombed in the Slidell family vault at St. Mark's Church in New York City, with full military honors. Two hundred marines, as well as many of Perry's former crewmen, friends, family, and admirers, escorted his body to the cemetery. Eight years after his death, Perry was moved from New York City to Island

Commodore Perry was moved to Island Cemetery in Newport, Rhode Island, in 1866. The inscription *(inset)* reads, "Erected by his widow to the memory of Matthew Calbraith Perry, Commodore in the U.S. Navy."

Cemetery in Newport, Rhode Island, where he had wished to be buried. The weather at the time of his death had prevented his burial in his birthplace.

Outside of New York and his circle of friends and family, there was little public attention paid to the passing of one of America's greatest naval heroes. Although the Old Bruin was no longer front-page news, Perry's friend James Watson Webb paid him a fitting tribute in the *Morning Courier and New York Enquirer*.

This monument of Perry stands in the Shimoda port in Shizuoka, Japan. It commemorates the arrival of Perry and the East India Squadron. Shimoda also celebrates the event with an annual parade, in which U.S. sailors and Japanese wear nineteenth-century clothing.

He described Perry as "a model of a naval officer, scrupulously exact in his discipline, and thoroughly American in all his views. . . . He had the valor of a hero and the capacity of a statesman, but both were outshone by a magnanimous heart which beat only to the measures of generosity and justice."

Timeline

1794   Matthew James Calbraith Perry is born in Newport, Rhode Island, on April 10.

1809   Perry becomes a midshipman in the U.S. Navy.

1809–1810   Perry serves on the ship *Revenge* under the command of his older brother, Oliver Hazard Perry.

1811   The *Little Belt* incident occurs while Perry is serving on board the *President*.

1812   Congress declares war on Great Britain.

1813   Perry is promoted to the rank of lieutenant.

1814   Perry marries Jane Slidell while on shore leave.

1816–1819   Perry is on furlough from the navy and serves as captain on a number of merchant vessels.

1819–1820   Perry returns to active duty on board the *Cyane*. He escorts the first ship of African American colonists back to Africa.

1821–1823   Perry is given command of the *Shark*. After bringing Reverend Ayers to Monrovia, Perry sails African waters looking for illegal slave ships. He then turns eastward and sails to the Caribbean to hunt pirates.

1824   Perry is first lieutenant on the ship *North Carolina*. He sails to the Mediterranean to protect American commercial shipping interests.

1827   As commander of the Boston Navy Yard, Perry begins his career as a naval reformer.

1830	Perry receives command of the sloop *Concord* as part of the Mediterranean Squadron.
1832	Perry helps to settle disagreements between the U.S. government and the Kingdom of the Two Sicilies.
1833	Perry returns to New York to become captain of the navy yard and recruiting station. He continues his activities as a reformer, building the steam navy and pushing for education.
1837	Perry takes command of the steamship *Fulton II*.
1841	Perry becomes commodore of the New York Navy Yard.
1842	The *Somers* mutiny occurs.
1843	Perry becomes commodore of the Africa Squadron. He polices the slave trade and settles disputes between African American settlers in Africa and African tribal leaders.
	The incident at Little Berebee occurs while Perry is investigating an attack on the *Mary Carver*.
1846	As commanding officer of the *Mississippi* and vice commodore of Gulf Squadron, Perry launches the first expedition to Tabasco during the Mexican War.
1847	Perry becomes commodore of the Gulf Squadron. He takes Veracruz and launches a successful second expedition to Tabasco.
1852	Perry is given command of the East India Squadron with the job of organizing an expedition to Japan.
1853	Perry arrives in Japan with official letters from President Fillmore. He negotiates with Japanese government officials and then leaves for Hong Kong.
1854	After about six months, Perry returns to Japan to conclude treaty negotiations. He signs the Treaty of Kanagawa that opens Japan to foreign trade.

1856	The first volume of the *Narrative of the Expedition of an American Squadron to the China Seas and Japan* is published.
1858	Commodore Perry dies at his home in New York at age sixty-three on March 4. He is buried in the Slidell family vault at St. Mark's Church in New York City.
1866	Perry's remains are moved to Island Cemetery in Newport, Rhode Island.

Glossary

abolitionists (a-buh-LIH-shun-ists) People who worked to end slavery.

batteries (BA-tuh-reez) Groups of artillery pieces or the guns on a warship.

blockade (blah-KAYD) To use a group of ships to block passage to ports by ships of another country.

brigade (brih-GAYD) A large body of troops.

communal (kuh-MYOO-nal) Owned by a group of people or community.

cosmopolitan (koz-muh-PAH-lih-tan) Having worldwide rather than local qualities.

deserters (dih-ZURT-erz) People who run away while serving with the military.

detachment (dih-TACH-ment) A group of soldiers or ships sent separately from the whole group for a special mission.

dey (DAY) A ruling official of the Ottoman Empire in northern Africa.

East Indies (EEST IN-deez) The old name for Indonesia and Southeast Asia.

engaged (in-GAYJD) Took part in.

flagship (FLAG-ship) A ship that carries the commander of a group of ships and that flies his or her flag.

flotilla (floh-TIH-luh) A large number of ships sailing together.

freedmen (FREED-men) People freed from slavery.

furlough (FUR-loh) A vacation for a soldier.

gunnery (GUN-ree) The study and practice of using artillery.

impressment (im-PRES-ment) The act of forcing someone into service.

khedive (keh-DEEV) The title of Turkish officials who governed Egypt in the nineteenth century.

militia (muh-LIH-shuh) A group of volunteer or citizen soldiers who are organized to assemble in emergencies.

missionaries (MIH-shuh-ner-eez) People sent to do religious work in a foreign country.

morale (muh-RAL) The mental and emotional feeling of a person or a group about the task at hand.

narrative (NAR-uh-tiv) A story.

pacifism (PA-sih-fih-zum) Refusal to use rough or harmful actions.

palavers (puh-LA-verz) Conferences or discussions between persons of different ranks or cultures.

persecution (per-sih-KYOO-shun) The act of attacking because of one's race or beliefs.

privateer (pry-vuh-TEER) A ship that is privately owned but given permission by a country to attack enemy ships in time of war.

repatriating (ree-PAY-tree-ayt-ing) Returning someone to their homeland.

samurai (SA-muh-ry) A kind of warrior who worked for the ruling class of Japan until the twentieth century.

seafaring (SEE-fer-ing) Having to do with sea travel.

shoguns (SHOH-gunz) Military chiefs who ruled Japan for nine centuries.

steerage (STIR-ij) The section of a ship below the main deck in the back, near the rudder.

Tokugawa (toh-koo-GAH-wah) The military family that ruled Japan from 1603 until 1868.

Additional Resources

To learn more about Commodore Matthew Perry, check out the following books and Web sites:

Books

Blumberg, Rhoda. *Commodore Perry in the Land of the Shogun.* New York: Lothrop, Lee & Shepard Books, 2003.

Icenhower, Joseph Bryan. *Perry and the Open Door to Japan: an American Commander Ends Centuries of Japanese Isolation.* New York: F. Watts, 1973.

Wiley, Peter Booth. *Yankees in the Land of the Gods: Commodore Perry and the Opening of Japan.* New York: Viking, 1990.

Web Sites

Due to the changing nature of Internet links, PowerPlus Books has developed an online list of Web sites related to the subject of this book. This site is updated regularly. Please use this link to access the list: www.powerkidslinks.com/lalt/mperry/

Bibliography

Barrows, Edward Morley. *Great Commodore: The Exploits of Matthew Calbraith Perry*. Indianapolis: The Bobbs-Merrill Co., 1935.

Copes, Jan M. "The Perry Family: a Newport Naval Dynasty of the Early Republic." *Newport History* 227 (Fall 1994): 48B77.

Kuhn, Ferdinand. *Commodore Perry and the Opening of Japan*. New York: Random House, 1955.

Morison, Samuel Eliot. *"Old Bruin": Commodore Matthew C. Perry, 1794–1858*. Boston: Little, Brown & Co., 1967.

Reynolds, Robert L. *Commodore Perry in Japan*. New York: American Heritage Publishing Co., 1963.

Schroeder, John H. *Matthew Calbraith Perry: Antebellum Sailor and Diplomat*. Annapolis, MD: Naval Institute Press, 2001.

Zabriskie, George A. "Commodore Matthew Calbraith Perry." *New-York Historical Society Quarterly* (Oct. 1946): 5B17.

Index

About the Author

David G. Wittner is an assistant professor of East Asian history and the chair of social sciences at Utica College in Utica, New York. He received his PhD from Ohio State University. He has published articles on the history of the Japanese iron and silk industries in English and Japanese. Wittner is a specialist in the history of Japanese technology.

Primary Sources

Cover (portrait). *Commodore Matthew Perry.* oil on canvas, 1834, William Sidney Mount, U.S. Naval Academy Museum. **Cover (background).** *Commodore Perry's Paddle-steamer Arriving in a Japanese Bay.* Woodblock print, undated, anonymous, British Museum, London/Bridgeman Art Library. **Page 4.** *Commodore Perry.* Daguerreotype, between 1854 and 1858, Mathew Brady, Library of Congress Prints and Photographs Division. **Page 6.** *Quaker Meeting.* Oil-on-canvas painting, 1849, English School, © Museum of Fine Arts, Boston/Bridgeman Art Library. **Page 10.** Map of Newport, Rhode Island. Hand-colored engraving, 1777, William Faden, Library of Congress Geography and Map Division. **Page 12.** *Oliver Hazard Perry.* Oil-on-canvas painting, 1813 or 1814, Rembrandt Peale, © New-York Historical Society/Bridgeman Art Library. **Page 17.** *Commodore John Rodgers.* Oil-on-canvas painting, 1818 or 1819, Charles Willson Peale, Independence National Historical Park. **Page 22.** *The U.S.S.* Chesapeake *approaching the H.M.S.* Shannon, *during the War of 1812.* Painting, 1813, Robert Dodd, Library of Congress Prints and Photographs Division. **Pages 24–25.** *Decatur's Squadron at Algiers.* Painting, 1815, John Bevan Irwin, The Mariners' Museum, Newport News, VA. **Page 28.** Congressional Act, 1819, National Archives and Records Administration. **Page 30.** Map of Africa. Hand-colored, 1820, Adrien Hubert Brué, Library of Congress Geography and Map Division. **Page 32.** The Liberian Senate. Watercolor and graphite on paper, circa 1856, Robert K. Griffin, Library of Congress Prints and Photographs Division. **Page 33.** Abolitionist print. Engraving, circa 1830, anonymous, Library of Congress Prints and Photographs Division. **Page 35.** *U.S. Schoner* (Schooner) *Shark Crossing the Bar Off Lisbon.* Watercolor on paper, late nineteenth century, J. Evans, Courtesy U.S. Navy Art Collection. **Page 36.** Map of Florida Keys and Key West. 1780, The Mariners' Museum, Newport News, VA. **Page 39.** *Triumphant Return of the American Squadron, Under Com. Bainbridge from the Mediterranean.* Engraving, 1816, After drawing by E. Tisdale, Library of Congress Prints and Photographs Division. **Page 41.** Naval Academy, Anapolis, MD. Colored engraving, circa 1855, W. R. Miller, courtesy, U.S. Naval Historical Center. **Page 42.** Map of the Mediterranean. Hand-colored engraving, 1817, Thompson, Library of Congress Geography and Map Division. **Page 45.** "Thoughts on the Navy." January 1837 issue of *Naval Magazine*, Matthew Calbraith Perry, Library of Congress, Rare Book and Special Collections Division. **Page 46.** *U.S. Naval*

Steamer Fulton. Lithograph on paper, circa 1831, S. McElroy, The Mariners' Museum, Newport News, VA. **Page 49.** *Abel P. Upshur*. Oil on canvas, 1893, A. G. Heaton, Courtesy U.S. Navy Art Collection. **Page 53.** Dr. Holt's Prescription for the Treatment of Yellow Fever. 1843, Library of Congress, Rare Book and Special Collections Division. **Page 54.** *Fish Town at Bassau, Liberia*. Watercolor, circa 1856, Robert K. Griffin, Library of Congress Prints and Photographs Division. **Page 60.** Map of the United States and Mexico. Engraving, 1845 published 1851, map drawn and engraved by J. Rapkin illustrations by H. Warrren illustrations engraved by H. Warren, copied with permission from the collection of Randy K. Haynie Family Collection. **Page 63.** *War News from Mexico*. Oil on canvas, 1848, Richard Caton Woodville, © Bettmann/CORBIS. **Page 66.** *General Winfield Scott*. Color lithograph, circa 1847, Currier & Ives, Library of Congress Prints and Photographs Division. **Page 68.** *The naval expedition under Commodore Perry, assending* [sic] *the Tabasco River at the Devils Bend—June 15th 1847*. Color lithograph, published circa 1848, Sarony & Major after the drawing by Lieutenant H. Walke, Library of Congress Prints and Photographs Division. **Page 72.** Tomb stone on the island of Amakusa. Photograph, Library of Congress Prints and Photographs Division. **Page 73.** Shogun rulers. Woodblock print, nineteenth century, Japanese School, Cragside House, Northumberland, UK, National Trust Photographic Library/Bridgeman Art Library. **Page 75.** *Steamboat, Possibly the U.S.S. Susquehanna, landing at Kurihama, Japan, July 8, 1853*. Watercolor, Library of Congress Prints and Photographs Division. **Page 76.** *Napha from the Sea*. Lithograph, 1856, W. Heine, Library of Congress Prints and Photographs Division. **Page 78.** *Young Samurai*. Hand-colored albumen print, late nineteenth century, unknown Japanese photographer, courtesy of Barry Chanders. **Page 81.** Mountains and coastline, from '36 Views of Mount Fuji'. Woodblock print, published 1853, Andō Hiroshige (Utagawa), Private Collection/Bridgeman Art Library. **Page 82.** Map of Japan. Hand-colored map, 1855, Joseph Hutchins Colton, Library of Congress Geography and Map Division. **Pages 88–89.** Landing of Commodore Perry at Yokahama. Hand-colored lithograph, 1854, W. Heine, engraved by E. Brown Jr., courtesy, U.S. Naval Historical Center. **Page 90.** The United States–Japan Treaty of Peace and Friendship (Treaty of Kanagawa). 1854, National Archives and Records Administration. **Page 94.** *A North American: Portrait of Perry*. Woodblock print, circa 1854, Library of Congress Prints and Photographs Division. **Page 95.** Perry medal. Bronze, twentieth century restrike of circa 1856 original, Francis N. Mitchell, courtesy of George C. Baxley. **Page 97.** Commodore Perry Headstone in Newport, Rhode Island. 1858, photo by Kim Fuller, Middletown, RI **Page 98.** Monument for the Arrival of Commodore Perry's Squadron, © Katsuji Iwao/Pacific Press Service.

Credits

Photo Credits

Cover, p. 85 courtesy U.S. Naval Academy Museum; cover (background) British Museum, London/Bridgeman Art Library; pp. 4, 22, 32, 33, 39, 54, 66, 68, 72, 75, 76, 94 Library of Congress Prints and Photographs Division; p. 6 © Museum of Fine Arts, Boston/Bridgeman Art Library; pp. 9, 81 Private Collection/Bridgeman Art Library; pp. 10, 30, 42, 82 Library of Congress Geography and Map Division; p. 12 © New-York Historical Society/Bridgeman Art Library; p. 15 U.S.S. Constitution Museum, Boston, MA; p. 17 Independence National Historical Park; pp. 20-21, 35, 49 Courtesy U.S. Navy Art Collection; pp. 24-25, 36, 46 The Mariners' Museum, Newport News, VA; pp. 28, 90 National Archives and Records Administration; pp. 41, 88-89 courtesy, U.S. Naval Historical Center; pp. 45, 53 Library of Congress, Rare Book and Special Collections Division; p. 57 courtesy U.S. Marine Corps Art Collection; p. 60 Copied with permission from the collection of Randy K. Haynie Family Collection; p. 63 © Bettmann/CORBIS; p. 73 Cragside House, Northumberland, UK, National Trust Photographic Library/Bridgeman Art Library; p. 78 courtesy of Barry Chanders; p. 95 courtesy of George C. Baxley; p. 97 photo by Kim Fuller, Middletown, RI; p. 98 © Katsuji Iwao/Pacific Press Service.

Project Editor

Jennifer Way

Series Design

Laura Murawski

Layout Design

Ginny Chu, Corinne L. Jacob

Photo Researcher

Jeffrey Wendt

JASPER COUNTY MIDDLE/HIGH SCHOOL
1289 College Street
Monticello, GA 31064